AI INVESTING: UNLEASHING THE POWER OF ARTIFICIAL INTELLIGENCE IN FINANCIAL MARKETS

PROF. BARCLAY NEWTON

Table of contents

- Sentiment analysis and news-based strategies.
- High-frequency trading and AI-driven market making.

CHAPTER FOUR: AI IN PORTFOLIO MANAGEMENT.
- Modern portfolio theory and AI optimization.
- Risk management and portfolio diversification using AI.
- Tactical asset allocation strategies with AI.
- Robo-advisors and AI-driven portfolio platforms.

CHAPTER FIVE: CHALLENGES AND ETHICAL CONSIDERATIONS.
- Limitations and pitfalls of AI investing.
- Algorithmic biases and fairness concerns.
- Regulatory considerations and transparency in AI investing.
- Balancing human judgment and AI-driven decisions.

CHAPTER SIX: REAL-WORLD CASE STUDIES.
- Case studies of successful AI investing applications.
- Balancing human judgment and AI-driven decisions.
- Lessons learned from AI-driven investment firms
- Examples of AI-driven trading systems and platforms.

CHAPTER SEVEN: FUTURE TRENDS AND OPPORTUNITIES.

- Advances in AI and machine learning for investing
- The Role of big data and alternative data sources
- AI-powered predictive analytics in financial markets
- The potential impact of blockchain and cryptocurrencies on AI investing

CONCLUSION..

APPENDIX

INTRODUCTION.

THE RISE OF AI AND ITS IMPACT ON THE FINANCIAL INDUSTRY.

The rise of AI has significantly impacted the financial world, revolutionizing investment decision-making. AI algorithms analyze vast amounts of data, identify patterns, and generate insights, leading to improved accuracy, efficiency, and potential for better returns in areas like stock trading, portfolio management, and risk assessment.

WHY AI INVESTING IS GAINING POPULARITY.

AI investing is gaining popularity due to several key factors. First, AI algorithms can process and analyze vast amounts of data quickly and efficiently, providing insights that human traders may miss. Second, AI algorithms can remove emotional biases from decision-making, leading to more objective and disciplined investment strategies. Lastly, advancements in AI technology and increased accessibility to AI tools and platforms have made it easier for individual investors to participate in AI-driven investing.

OVERVIEW OF THE BOOK'S OBJECTIVES.

The objective of this book is to provide readers with a comprehensive understanding of AI investing in the financial markets. It aims to explore the principles, techniques, and applications of AI in investment decision-making. By examining different strategies, challenges, and ethical considerations, the book seeks to equip readers with the knowledge and insights necessary to leverage AI effectively in their investment endeavors. Real-world case studies and future trends are also explored to offer practical guidance and spark innovative thinking in the evolving landscape of AI investing.

CHAPTER ONE.

UNDERSTANDING AI IN INVESTING.

WHAT IS AI AND HOW IS IT APPLIED IN THE FINANCIAL MARKET?

AI, or artificial intelligence, encompasses techniques that enable machines to mimic human intelligence. In financial markets, AI can be applied to analyze vast data sets, identify patterns, and make data-driven predictions. It assists in investment decision-making, risk assessment, portfolio optimization, and automated trading strategies.

THE BENEFITS AND CHALLENGES OF AI INVESTING.

AI in investing brings significant benefits and challenges. It enhances decision-making by analyzing vast amounts of data, automates tasks, and excels at pattern recognition. However, challenges include data quality and bias, interpretability of complex models, and ethical considerations. Striking a balance is crucial for successful AI integration in investment practices.

DIFFERENT TYPES OF AI ALGORITHMS USED IN INVESTING.

There are various types of AI algorithms used in investing. Here are some commonly employed ones:

1. **Supervised Learning**: This algorithm learns from labeled historical data, where inputs (e.g., financial indicators) are mapped to corresponding outputs (e.g., buy/sell signals). It can be used for stock price prediction and classification tasks.

2. **Unsupervised Learning**: This algorithm analyzes unlabeled data to discover patterns, relationships, and clusters. It is useful for data exploration, anomaly detection, and portfolio segmentation.

3. **Reinforcement Learning:** This algorithm learns through trial and error interactions with an environment. It aims to maximize rewards by making sequential decisions. Reinforcement learning can be applied to optimize trading strategies and portfolio rebalancing.

4. **Natural Language Processing (NLP):** NLP algorithms process and understand human language. In investing, NLP is used to analyze news articles, social media sentiment, and corporate filings for sentiment analysis, news-based trading signals, and event-driven investing.

5. **Genetic Algorithms**: Inspired by the process of natural selection, genetic algorithms evolve and

optimize trading strategies by iteratively selecting, combining, and mutating potential solutions.

CHAPTER TWO.

FOUNDATIONS OF AI INVESTING

DATA COLLECTION AND PREPROCESSING OF AI MODELS.

Data collection and preprocessing are essential steps in preparing data for AI models in investing.

Data Collection:

Data collection involves identifying relevant data sources and accessing the necessary data for the AI model. This may include financial market data, company financials, news feeds, and social media sentiment. Ensuring data quality and accuracy is crucial during this stage.

Data Preprocessing:

Data preprocessing involves several key steps:

1. **Data cleaning**: Removing or correcting erroneous or missing data points and handling outliers to ensure data integrity.

2. **Feature selection:** Choosing the most relevant features or variables that will serve as inputs for the AI model. This selection is based on factors that have the greatest impact on the target variable or investment decision.

3. **Feature engineering:** Creating new features or transforming existing ones to extract meaningful information. This may involve calculations, aggregations, or transformations to enhance the predictive power of the AI model.

4. **Data normalization:** Scaling the data to a common range to ensure variables with different units or scales have a comparable impact on the AI model's performance.

5. **Splitting the data:** Dividing the dataset into training, validation, and testing sets. The training set is used to train the AI model, the validation set helps tune model parameters, and the testing set evaluates the model's performance on unseen data.

By performing data collection and preprocessing effectively, AI models receive clean, relevant, and properly formatted data. This sets the foundation for accurate and effective training and evaluation, ultimately improving the quality and performance of AI models in making investment decisions.

FEATURE ENGINEERING AND SELECTION.

Feature engineering is the process of creating new or transforming existing ones to extract valuable information from the raw data. It involves performing calculations, aggregations, or transformations to generate input variables that are more predictive of the target variable or investment decision.

Feature selection, on the other hand, is about choosing the most relevant features to include in the AI model. It aims to identify the factors that have the most impact on the target variable while removing any redundant or irrelevant features. This helps simplify the model and improve its performance by focusing on the most meaningful information.

BUILDING AND TRAINING AI INVESTMENT MODELS.

The process of building and training AI investment models involves several important steps. First, we need to clearly define the investment problem we want to solve, like predicting stock prices or optimizing portfolios. Then, we gather relevant data from different sources and prepare it by cleaning and selecting the most important features.

Next, we choose the right AI model for our problem, which could be a model that predicts outcomes or learns patterns from data. We train the model using our prepared data, adjusting its parameters to improve its performance.

After training, we validate and evaluate the model to see how well it performs. We assess its accuracy or other metrics that matter for our investment problem. Based on the results, we refine the model to make it better.

Once we're satisfied with the model's performance, we test it on new data to simulate real-world scenarios. If it works well, we can use the model to make investment decisions manually or through automated systems.

It's important to remember that we should continuously monitor and update the model as market conditions change and new data becomes available. This ensures that our AI investment model remains effective and aligned with our investment goals.

BACK TESTING AND PERFORMANCE EVALUATION.

Backtesting and performance evaluation are crucial steps in assessing the effectiveness of AI investment models.

Backtesting: Backtesting involves testing the AI investment model on historical data to evaluate its performance. It simulates how the model would have performed if it had been used in the past. By comparing the model's predictions or trading decisions with actual historical outcomes, we can assess its accuracy and effectiveness.

Performance Evaluation: Performance evaluation is the process of measuring and analyzing the performance of the AI investment model. It involves evaluating various metrics, such as accuracy, profitability, risk-adjusted returns, or other relevant indicators. This helps us understand how well the model has performed in achieving its intended investment objectives.

During backtesting and performance evaluation, it is important to use out-of-sample data that the model has not seen during training. This ensures that the evaluation is conducted on unseen data, providing a more realistic assessment of the model's performance in real-world scenarios.

By conducting thorough backtesting and performance evaluation, we can gain insights into the strengths and weaknesses of the AI investment model. This information can guide us in refining the model, improving its performance, and making informed decisions about its practical implementation in investment strategies.

CHAPTER THREE.

AI STRATEGIES FOR STOCK INVESTING.

FUNDAMENTAL ANALYSIS USING AI TECHNIQUES.

Fundamental analysis is an investment approach that focuses on understanding the true value of stocks or securities. When combined with AI techniques, it can be even more powerful. With AI, investors can gather and analyze a lot of financial data more efficiently. They can use AI to read and understand news articles and economic indicators. AI can also identify patterns and trends in the data that are hard for humans to spot. By using AI, investors can make better predictions about how companies will perform in the future and assess the level of risk. They can also optimize their investment portfolios based on their goals and market conditions. Overall, AI enhances fundamental analysis by providing deeper insights and helping investors make smarter investment decisions.

TECHNICAL ANALYSIS AND PATTERN RECOGNITION.

Technical analysis is an investment approach that focuses on studying historical market data, such as price and volume, to predict future price movements and make investment decisions. Pattern recognition is a key component of technical analysis. It involves identifying recurring patterns or trends in the market data, such as chart patterns or indicators, that can provide insights into future price behavior. By recognizing these patterns, investors can make informed decisions about when to buy or sell securities. Pattern recognition techniques are often enhanced with AI algorithms, which can analyze large amounts of data and identify patterns more accurately and efficiently than human analysts.

SENTIMENT ANALYSIS AND NEWS-BASED STRATEGIES.

Sentiment analysis is a technique used in investment strategies to analyze the sentiment or emotions expressed in news articles, social media posts, or other textual data. It aims to gauge the overall positive or negative sentiment surrounding a particular asset, company, or market.

By applying AI and natural language processing (NLP) techniques, sentiment analysis can automatically extract sentiment-related information from large volumes of text. AI algorithms can identify keywords, phrases, and contextual cues to determine whether the sentiment is positive, negative, or neutral.

News-based strategies leverage sentiment analysis to make investment decisions. Positive sentiment might indicate a favorable market outlook or a positive perception of a company, influencing investors to consider buying or holding the asset. Conversely, negative sentiment might trigger selling or avoiding certain investments.

Sentiment analysis can provide valuable insights into market sentiment, helping investors identify trends, anticipate market reactions, and adjust their investment strategies accordingly. However, it's important to note that sentiment analysis is just one factor to consider in investment decisions and should be used in conjunction with other fundamental and technical analysis techniques.

HIGH-FREQUENCY TRADING AND AI-DRIVEN MARKET MAKING.

High-frequency trading (HFT) is a strategy that utilizes powerful computers and algorithms to execute a large number of trades in milliseconds. It relies on speed, sophisticated algorithms, and co-location proximity to exchanges to take advantage of small price discrepancies or market inefficiencies. HFT aims to profit from short-term price movements and market liquidity.

AI-driven market trading, on the other hand, involves the use of artificial intelligence techniques to make trading decisions. AI algorithms analyze vast amounts of data, including market trends, historical prices, news sentiment, and other relevant factors, to identify patterns and generate trading signals. These signals can be used to execute trades automatically or assist human traders in their decision-making process.

The combination of AI and high-frequency trading has the potential to enhance trading strategies by incorporating advanced machine learning models and predictive analytics. AI can process large datasets in real time and adapt to changing market conditions, improving trading accuracy and speed. It can also help identify hidden patterns or correlations that may not be apparent to human traders.

However, it's important to note that HFT and AI-driven market trading come with their risks and challenges. They can contribute to increased market volatility and create a complex trading environment. Regulatory concerns, technical issues, and potential market manipulation are factors that need to be carefully considered.

Overall, HFT and AI-driven market trading has revolutionized the trading landscape, introducing automation and advanced data analysis techniques. These approaches continue to evolve, and market participants need to stay abreast of the latest developments and regulatory requirements to navigate the dynamic nature of these trading strategies effectively.

CHAPTER FOUR.

AI IN PORTFOLIO MANAGEMENT.

MODERN PORTFOLIO THEORY AND AI OPTIMIZATION.

Modern Portfolio Theory (MPT) is an investment developed by Harry Markowitz that aims to maximize portfolio returns while minimizing risk. It emphasizes the importance of diversification and the efficient allocation of assets.

AI optimization techniques can enhance the application of MPT by utilizing advanced algorithms to optimize portfolio construction and asset allocation. These techniques analyze large sets of historical data, market trends, and risk-return profiles of different assets to identify optimal portfolio allocations.

AI optimization algorithms can consider various factors, including historical asset returns, correlations, risk measures, and investor preferences. They can generate efficient frontiers that represent the optimal trade-off between risk and return for different asset allocation strategies. By incorporating AI optimization, investors can identify portfolios that offer better risk-adjusted returns and potentially outperform traditional portfolio construction methods.

AI optimization techniques can also adapt to changing market conditions and incorporate real-time data, allowing for dynamic portfolio adjustments. This flexibility helps investors capture market opportunities and manage risk more effectively.

However, it's important to note that AI optimization is not a guarantee of success. It relies on the quality of data, the accuracy of assumptions, and the appropriate calibration of algorithms. Additionally, it should be used alongside careful consideration of individual investment goals, risk tolerance, and market conditions.

In summary, AI optimization techniques can complement Modern Portfolio Theory by providing more sophisticated and data-driven approaches to portfolio construction and asset allocation. They offer the potential to improve risk-adjusted returns and adapt to changing market dynamics, but prudent oversight and consideration of investor-specific factors are essential for successful implementation.

RISK MANAGEMENT AND PORTFOLIO DIVERSIFICATION USING AI.

Risk management and portfolio diversification are crucial aspects of investment strategies, and AI can play a significant role in enhancing these practices.

Risk Management: AI can help identify, assess, and manage risks in investment portfolios. By analyzing historical data and market trends, AI algorithms can identify potential risks and their potential impact on portfolio performance. AI can also assist in stress testing portfolios under different scenarios to assess their resilience to adverse market conditions. Additionally, AI techniques can be employed to implement risk mitigation strategies, such as dynamic asset allocation or hedging techniques, to reduce exposure to specific risks.

Portfolio Diversification: AI can enhance portfolio diversification by analyzing vast amounts of data and identifying non-obvious correlations and relationships among assets. By leveraging machine learning algorithms, AI can identify asset classes or securities that exhibit low correlation with each other, helping to build diversified portfolios that can potentially reduce overall risk. AI can also assist in optimizing portfolio weights and allocations based on risk-return objectives, constraints, and market conditions, ensuring an optimal balance between diversification and expected returns.

Furthermore, AI can continuously monitor portfolio performance, risk exposure, and market conditions in real time. This enables proactive risk management and timely adjustments to portfolio allocations as market conditions evolve.

It's important to note that while AI can provide valuable insights and assist in risk management and portfolio diversification, human judgment and expertise remain essential. Investors should interpret AI-generated insights within the context of their investment goals, risk tolerance, and market understanding. Additionally, thorough validation and ongoing monitoring of AI models are necessary to ensure their effectiveness and reliability in managing risk and diversifying portfolios.

TACTICAL ASSETS ALLOCATION STRATEGIES WITH AI.

Tactical asset allocation strategies involve making short-term adjustments to a portfolio based on changing market conditions. With AI, these strategies can be enhanced using advanced algorithms and data analysis.

AI can analyze large amounts of data, like market indicators and news sentiment, to identify patterns and trends that humans might miss. It can also forecast market movements and make real-time adjustments to the portfolio based on those predictions.

By using AI in tactical asset allocation, investors can potentially take advantage of short-term opportunities and manage risks more effectively. However, it's important to note that human oversight and decision-making are still essential when interpreting AI-generated insights and aligning them with individual investment goals and risk preferences.

ROBO ADVISORS AND AI-DRIVEN PORTFOLIO PLATFORMS.

Robo advisors and AI-driven portfolio platforms are technology-driven investment platforms that utilize AI algorithms to provide automated and personalized investment services. Here's a brief explanation:

Robo Advisors: Robo advisors are online platforms that use AI algorithms to offer automated investment advice and portfolio management. They gather information from investors about their financial goals, risk tolerance, and investment preferences. Using this data, along with algorithms and models, robo-advisors recommend and manage portfolios of diversified investments, typically consisting of exchange-traded funds (ETFs) or mutual funds. Robo advisors often provide low-cost and accessible investment solutions, making investing more convenient for individuals who may not have extensive investment knowledge or large capital to invest.

AI-Driven Portfolio Platforms: AI-driven portfolio platforms are advanced investment platforms that leverage AI algorithms and data analytics to provide portfolio management services. These platforms analyze large volumes of data, including market trends, economic indicators, and investor behavior, to generate investment insights and optimize portfolio allocations. AI algorithms help in identifying investment opportunities, managing risk, and making real-time adjustments to portfolios based on market conditions. These platforms often offer more sophisticated and tailored investment strategies, catering to investors with varying risk profiles and investment goals.

Both robo-advisors and AI-driven portfolio platforms aim to simplify the investment process, automate portfolio management, and provide personalized investment advice. They can be particularly beneficial for individuals seeking cost-effective and convenient investment solutions, as well as for those who value data-driven insights and real-time portfolio adjustments. However, investors need to consider their own financial goals, risk tolerance, and the level of control they desire when choosing between robo-advisors and AI-driven portfolio platforms.

CHAPTER FIVE

CHALLENGES AND ETHICAL CONSIDERATIONS.

THE LIMITATIONS AND PITFALLS OF AI INVESTING.

While AI investing has its advantages, it also has limitations and pitfalls to consider.

AI investing has some drawbacks that investors should be aware of. Firstly, AI models heavily rely on historical data, so if the data is incomplete or biased, it can lead to inaccurate predictions. Overfitting is another concern, where AI models perform well on historical data but struggle with new situations. Additionally, AI may lack the human judgment and intuition that human investors possess, limiting their ability to adapt to unique market conditions.

Financial markets are complex, and AI may not always capture the nuances or anticipate unexpected events. The reliance on historical patterns may not account for changes in the market, and there can be regulatory and ethical considerations surrounding AI investing.

To navigate these limitations, investors need to approach AI investing with a critical mindset. Combining AI capabilities with human judgment can help mitigate risks. By staying informed and actively overseeing AI models, investors can make more informed investment decisions.

Overall, while AI can provide valuable insights, it's essential to recognize its limitations and use it as a tool alongside human expertise.

ALGORITHMIC BIASES AND FAIRNESS CONCERNS.

Algorithmic biases and fairness concerns are significant considerations when utilizing AI in investing.

Algorithmic Biases: AI algorithms learn from historical data, and if that data is biased, it can lead to biased outcomes. Biases in data can perpetuate unfair practices and discrimination, impacting investment decisions and outcomes. It is crucial to carefully assess and address biases to ensure fair treatment of investors.

Fairness Concerns: AI algorithms may unintentionally perpetuate unfair outcomes or reinforce existing disparities. For example, if historical data reflects societal biases, AI models may replicate those biases, leading to unequal access or opportunities in investing. Fairness concerns arise when certain groups are disadvantaged or excluded due to algorithmic decision-making.

Addressing Biases and Promoting Fairness: To mitigate algorithmic biases and promote fairness, it is necessary to conduct rigorous data analysis, identify and remove biased attributes, and continuously evaluate and refine AI models. Transparency in algorithms and the decision-making process is also crucial to understanding and addressing potential biases. Additionally, diverse and inclusive teams working on AI development can help bring different perspectives and reduce biases.

Regulatory Attention: Regulators are increasingly focusing on algorithmic fairness and biases in AI systems. There are ongoing discussions and efforts to establish guidelines and standards to ensure fair and ethical AI practices in the investment industry. Compliance with regulatory requirements and industry best practices is essential to mitigate risks and build trust.

Investors and organizations should prioritize fairness, ethical considerations, and accountability when utilizing AI in investing. Continuous monitoring, audits, and ongoing evaluation of AI systems can help identify and rectify biases, promoting fairness and ensuring a more equitable investment environment.

REGULATORY CONSIDERATIONS AND TRANSPARENCY IN AI INVESTING.

Regulatory Considerations: The use of AI in investing is subject to regulatory frameworks aimed at ensuring investor protection, market integrity, and fair practices. Regulatory bodies are increasingly focusing on AI-related risks, including algorithmic biases, data privacy, transparency, and compliance. Investors and organizations need to understand and comply with applicable regulations and guidelines to mitigate legal and compliance risks.

Transparency: Transparency is vital in AI investing to promote accountability and trust. Investors should have a clear understanding of how AI models are developed, the data used, and the underlying assumptions and limitations. Transparent disclosure of the use of AI in investment processes can help investors make informed decisions and assess the reliability and fairness of AI-driven recommendations.

Ethical Considerations: Alongside regulations, ethical considerations are critical in AI investing. Transparency regarding data collection, usage, and storage helps address privacy concerns. Fairness, avoiding discrimination, and addressing biases in AI models are also ethical imperatives. Organizations should establish clear ethical guidelines and adhere to responsible AI practices to ensure alignment with societal values and investor expectations.

Engagement with Regulators: To stay compliant, investors and organizations should actively engage with regulatory bodies and industry associations to stay informed about evolving regulatory requirements and industry best practices. Collaboration with regulators can help shape regulatory frameworks and address concerns related to AI in investing.

By adhering to regulatory requirements, embracing transparency, and considering ethical implications, AI in investing can be utilized responsibly. Transparent disclosure, robust governance frameworks, and ongoing monitoring and evaluation can help ensure that AI-driven investment processes are aligned with regulatory standards, promote transparency, and inspire investor confidence.

BALANCING HUMAN JUDGEMENT AND AI-DRIVEN DECISIONS.

Human Judgment: Human judgment brings unique qualities such as intuition, emotional intelligence, and contextual understanding to the investment decision-making process. Humans can consider qualitative factors, interpret complex market dynamics, and incorporate subjective insights that AI may struggle to capture. The human judgment also allows for flexibility, adaptability, and the ability to make decisions in unforeseen or uncertain situations.

AI-Driven Decision-Making: AI excels in processing vast amounts of data, identifying patterns, and making data-driven predictions. AI algorithms can analyze historical trends, assess market conditions, and provide quantitative insights with speed and accuracy. AI can uncover non-obvious correlations, detect market inefficiencies, and automate routine tasks, enhancing efficiency and scalability in investment processes.

Balancing the Two: To leverage the strengths of both human judgment and AI, it's essential to find a balance that maximizes their complementary advantages. This can be achieved by incorporating AI-driven insights into the decision-making process while allowing human judgment to provide the final assessment and validation. Human oversight ensures critical evaluation of AI-generated recommendations, considering factors beyond quantitative data.

Human-AI Collaboration: Collaboration between humans and AI systems is key to successful decision-making. Human experts can provide guidance, set strategic objectives, and define the constraints and ethical boundaries within which AI operates. Continuous monitoring, validation, and recalibration of AI models by human experts are essential to ensure their effectiveness and mitigate potential biases or errors.

Investor Considerations: Investors should consider their risk tolerance, investment goals, and personal preferences when determining the appropriate balance between human judgment and AI-driven decision-making. Some may prefer a more hands-on approach with human expertise at the forefront, while others may be more open to relying on AI-driven insights.

Finding the right balance between human judgment and AI-driven decision-making is a dynamic process that requires ongoing evaluation, refinement, and adaptability. By combining human judgment and AI capabilities, investors can benefit from the strengths of both approaches, enhancing decision-making processes and potentially improving investment outcomes.

CHAPTER SIX.

CASE STUDIES OF SUCCESSFUL AI INVESTING PLATFORMS.

There have been several successful AI-driven investing platforms that have demonstrated positive outcomes. Here are a few notable case studies:

1. **Wealthfront**: Wealthfront is a robo-advisor that utilizes AI algorithms to provide automated investment management services. Their platform uses AI to create and manage diversified portfolios of low-cost ETFs tailored to each investor's risk tolerance and financial goals. Wealthfront's AI-driven approach has attracted a large user base and has demonstrated consistent performance in generating competitive returns for investors.

2. **Sentient Technologies**: Sentient Technologies is an AI-driven investment firm that applies evolutionary algorithms and machine learning techniques to generate trading strategies. Their AI platform analyzes large amounts of financial data, identifies patterns, and adapts

strategies to changing market conditions. Sentient Technologies has reported positive returns in its trading activities, showcasing the potential of AI in the investment space.

3. **Kensho Technologies**: Kensho Technologies, now a part of S&P Global, developed an AI-powered analytics platform for financial markets. Their platform utilizes natural language processing and machine learning algorithms to extract and analyze data from news articles, research reports, and financial statements. By providing real-time insights and predictions, Kensho has been successful in assisting investment professionals in making more informed decisions.

These case studies highlight how AI-driven platforms have been successful in automating investment processes, optimizing portfolio management, and generating competitive returns. However, it's important to note that the performance of AI platforms can vary, and individual investor outcomes may differ. Conducting thorough research, understanding the underlying methodologies, and considering risk factors are essential when evaluating any AI-driven investing platform.

LESSONS LEARNED FROM AI-DRIVEN INVESTMENT FIRMS.

AI-driven investment firms have provided valuable lessons for the investment industry. Here are some key lessons learned:

1. **Embrace Data-driven Decision Making**: AI-driven investment firms have shown the power of leveraging vast amounts of data to make informed investment decisions. They emphasize the importance of data quality, data analysis, and utilizing sophisticated algorithms to extract valuable insights. This highlights the need for investment professionals to adapt to a data-driven mindset and incorporate advanced analytics into their decision-making processes.

2. **Continuous Learning and Adaptation**: Successful AI-driven investment firms understand the importance of continuous learning and adaptation. They continuously refine their models, algorithms, and strategies based on market conditions and performance feedback. This agile approach helps them stay responsive to changing market dynamics and optimize their investment strategies over time.

3. **Combining Human Expertise with AI**: AI-driven investment firms recognize that human expertise is still critical in the investment process. They emphasize the collaboration between human professionals and AI algorithms, where human judgment and domain

knowledge complement the capabilities of AI. This human-AI partnership enhances decision-making, risk management, and the ability to navigate complex market situations.

4. **Addressing Algorithmic Biases and Ethics**: AI-driven investment firms have highlighted the importance of addressing algorithmic biases and ethical considerations. They acknowledge the potential biases that can be embedded in AI models and the need to actively monitor, evaluate, and address these biases. Ethical guidelines and responsible AI practices are essential to ensure fairness, transparency, and compliance with regulatory requirements.

5. **Investor Education and Communication**: AI-driven investment firms understand the significance of investor education and communication. They invest in transparent reporting, clear explanations of their AI-driven strategies, and effective communication channels to build trust with investors. Educating investors about the benefits and limitations of AI in investing helps manage expectations and fosters long-term relationships.

6. **Regulatory Compliance and Risk Management**: AI-driven investment firms recognize the importance of regulatory compliance and robust risk management frameworks. They operate within regulatory boundaries, ensuring compliance with applicable laws and regulations. Risk management practices, including

stress testing, scenario analysis, and ongoing monitoring, are essential to mitigate risks associated with AI-driven investment strategies.

These lessons learned from AI-driven investment firms highlight the significance of combining human expertise with AI capabilities, embracing data-driven decision-making, addressing biases and ethical concerns, and ensuring regulatory compliance and risk management. Applying these lessons can help investors and investment professionals harness the potential of AI while navigating the challenges and complexities of the investment landscape.

CHAPTER SEVEN.

FUTURE TRENDS AND OPPORTUNITIES.

ADVANCES IN AI AND MACHINE LEARNING IN INVESTING.

The advancements of AI and machine learning in investing have transformed the way investment decisions are made. These are how AI has transformed the investment world:

1. **Enhanced Data Processing:** AI and machine learning algorithms have revolutionized data processing capabilities in investing. They can analyze vast amounts of financial data, news articles, social media sentiment, and other relevant information, extracting valuable insights and patterns that were previously challenging for human analysts to uncover.

2. **Improved Predictive Analytics:** AI and machine learning models have shown significant progress in predictive analytics. By leveraging historical data and sophisticated algorithms, these models can forecast market trends, identify investment opportunities, and make predictions about asset prices and market

movements with higher accuracy than traditional methods.

3. **Automation and Efficiency:** AI-driven tools and platforms have automated various aspects of investing, making processes more efficient and reducing manual efforts. Tasks such as portfolio optimization, trade execution, risk management, and performance monitoring can be automated, allowing investment professionals to focus on higher-level decision-making and strategic analysis.

4. **Alternative Data Integration:** AI and machine learning have enabled the integration of alternative data sources into investment analysis. Non-traditional data, such as satellite imagery, web scraping, and sensor data, can provide valuable insights into industries, consumer behavior, and market trends. AI algorithms can process and analyze this data, enhancing investment strategies and generating unique insights.

5. **Risk Management and Fraud Detection**: AI has improved risk management in investing by providing real-time monitoring and detection of potential risks and anomalies. Machine learning algorithms can identify patterns associated with fraud, market manipulation, and abnormal trading activities, enabling early detection and prevention of fraudulent activities.

6. **Personalized Investment Solutions:** AI-driven platforms can offer personalized investment solutions

tailored to individual investors' preferences, risk profiles, and financial goals. These platforms leverage machine learning algorithms to generate customized recommendations and portfolio allocations, providing investors with a more personalized and tailored investment experience.

7. **Reinforcement Learning and AI Agents:**
Advancements in reinforcement learning have allowed the development of AI agents that can learn and adapt their investment strategies through interactions with the market. These AI agents continuously improve their decision-making capabilities, optimize portfolio management, and adapt to changing market conditions.

The advancements in AI and machine learning have significantly impacted the investment industry, enabling more data-driven decision-making, automation, and personalized solutions. As AI continues to evolve, it is expected to further enhance investment strategies, risk management, and overall performance, offering new opportunities and challenges for investors and investment professionals.

THE ROLE OF BIG DATA AND ALTERNATIVE DATA SOURCES.

Big data and alternative data sources play a crucial role in modern investing by providing valuable insights and improving decision-making.

Big Data: Big data refers to the massive amount of information generated from various sources like financial markets, social media, and online platforms. In investing, big data offers benefits such as:

1. **Deeper Analysis:** Big data allows investors to analyze vast amounts of information to uncover patterns and trends that traditional data sources may miss.

2. **Real-time Insights:** Investors can monitor and analyze real-time market data and news to make informed decisions quickly.

3. **Better Models**: By incorporating big data into models, investors can build more accurate predictive models for investment strategies and risk management.

Alternative Data Sources: Alternative data refers to non-traditional information like satellite imagery and social media feeds. They contribute to investing in the following ways:

1. **Unique Insights:** Alternative data provides unconventional perspectives on market trends, consumer behavior, and industry dynamics.

2. **Early Trend Detection**: Alternative data can reveal early indicators of emerging trends, helping investors stay ahead of the curve.

Overall, big data and alternative data sources empower investors to gain deeper insights, make better-informed decisions, and potentially achieve a competitive advantage in the market.

AI-POWERED PREDICTIVE ANALYTICS IN FINANCIAL MARKETS.

1. **Data Analysis:** AI algorithms analyze vast amounts of historical and real-time financial data, including market prices, economic indicators, news articles, and social media sentiment. They identify patterns, correlations, and anomalies within the data to uncover valuable insights.

2. **Market Trend Forecasting:** AI models use historical data to identify and predict market trends. By analyzing patterns and relationships, they can provide predictions on the direction and momentum of various financial instruments, helping investors make informed decisions.

3. **Asset Price Prediction**: AI algorithms can forecast the future prices of stocks, bonds, commodities, and other assets. They analyze historical price data, technical indicators, and market factors to generate predictions, assisting investors in identifying potential buying or selling opportunities.

4. **Risk Assessment:** AI-powered predictive analytics assess risk by analyzing historical market data and factors that influence market volatility. They can help

investors estimate the potential risks associated with specific investments or portfolios, enabling better risk management strategies.

5. **Portfolio Optimization**: AI models optimize portfolio allocation by considering various factors such as risk tolerance, investment goals, and market conditions. They provide recommendations on optimal asset allocation to maximize returns while managing risk.

6. **Trading Strategy Development**: AI-driven predictive analytics help develop and refine trading strategies. By analyzing historical market data and identifying profitable patterns, algorithms can generate signals for buying or selling securities, supporting algorithmic trading and enhancing trading performance.

THE POTENTIAL IMPACT OF BLOCKCHAIN AND CRYPTOCURRENCIES ON AI INVESTING.

Blockchain and cryptocurrencies have the potential to revolutionize AI investing by offering enhanced data security, automated transactions, tokenization, and increased market access.

With blockchain technology, financial data can be securely stored and shared in a decentralized and tamper-proof manner, ensuring the integrity of AI models and predictions. Smart contracts enable automated and secure transactions, streamlining trade execution, settlement, and compliance processes.

Tokenization on the blockchain allows for the representation of assets as digital tokens, increasing liquidity and facilitating fractional ownership. AI algorithms can leverage these tokenized assets to create diversified investment portfolios and enable seamless trading of digital tokens.

Furthermore, blockchain and cryptocurrencies provide access to global markets by enabling fast and cost-effective cross-border transactions. AI models can analyze data from various markets, expanding investment opportunities and diversification potential.

Transparency is a key feature of blockchain technology, as all transactions are recorded on a public ledger. This enhances audibility and traceability, promoting trust and accountability in AI investing.

However, challenges such as regulatory considerations, scalability, and market volatility need to be addressed for the full potential of blockchain and cryptocurrencies in AI investing to be realized. Nonetheless, the intersection of AI, blockchain, and cryptocurrencies holds promise for transforming the way investments are made, making them more secure, efficient, and accessible to a broader range of investors.

CONCLUSION.

In summary, this book provides valuable insights into the intersection of artificial intelligence and the financial world. Here are the key takeaways:

AI is revolutionizing investing: AI algorithms and machine learning techniques are transforming the investment landscape by analyzing vast amounts of data, making predictions, and automating investment processes.

Benefits of AI investing: AI offers benefits such as enhanced data analysis, improved predictive analytics, automation of tasks, and personalized investment solutions. It enables investors to make more informed decisions, optimize portfolios, and identify market opportunities.

Challenges and limitations: AI investing has its limitations, including algorithmic biases, data quality concerns, and the need for human oversight. Understanding these challenges is essential for the effective and responsible use of AI in investing.

Data collection and preprocessing: Data collection and preprocessing are critical steps in building AI investment models. They involve gathering relevant data, cleaning and organizing it, and transforming it into a format suitable for analysis.

Algorithm selection and training: Different AI algorithms, such as regression models, neural networks, and decision trees, can be used in investment analysis. Training these models with historical data helps them learn patterns and make predictions.

Fundamental and technical analysis: AI can be applied to fundamental analysis by analyzing financial statements, news sentiment, and macroeconomic factors. It can also automate technical analysis, identifying patterns and trends in price charts.

Risk management and portfolio optimization: AI helps in risk management by monitoring market conditions, detecting anomalies, and optimizing portfolios based on risk-return profiles. It assists in diversification and managing downside risks.

Ethical and regulatory considerations: AI investing raises ethical concerns, such as algorithmic biases and fairness issues. Compliance with regulatory frameworks and ensuring transparency in AI-driven investment processes is crucial.

Future of AI in investing: This book explores emerging trends, including the impact of blockchain, cryptocurrencies, and alternative data sources on AI investing. It emphasizes the importance of continuous learning and adapting to advancements in technology.

APPENDIX

ABOUT THE AUTHOR

Prof. Barclay Newton is a renowned expert in the field of AI and finance. With over two decades of experience in the financial industry, Prof. Barclay has witnessed the transformative power of AI firsthand. As a researcher, author, and practitioner, he has dedicated his career to exploring the intersection of artificial intelligence and investing. Driven by his passion for technology and finance, he has developed innovative AI-driven investment strategies that have consistently delivered impressive results. With a knack for simplifying complex concepts, Prof. Barclay has a unique ability to communicate the intricacies of AI investing in a clear and accessible manner. His expertise and deep understanding of the subject make him a trusted authority in the field. Prof. Barclays' commitment to sharing knowledge and empowering others has made him a sought-after speaker at international conferences and a trusted advisor to financial institutions. Through his book, he aims to demystify AI investing, equip readers with practical insights, and inspire them to embrace the potential of AI in shaping the future of finance.

GLOSSARY OF KEY TERMS

Artificial Intelligence (AI): The field of computer science that focuses on creating intelligent machines capable of performing tasks that typically require human intelligence.

Machine Learning: A subset of AI that involves training algorithms to learn patterns and make predictions or take actions without explicit programming.

Data Preprocessing: The process of cleaning, transforming, and organizing raw data to make it suitable for analysis and modeling

Algorithm: A step-by-step procedure or set of rules followed to solve a specific problem. In AI investing, algorithms are used to analyze data and make investment decisions.

Predictive Analytics: The use of historical data and statistical techniques to make predictions about future outcomes.

Fundamental Analysis: An investment approach that evaluates the intrinsic value of a company or asset by analyzing financial statements, industry trends, and economic factors.

Technical Analysis: A method of evaluating investments by analyzing historical price and volume data, identifying patterns, and making predictions based on market trends.

Risk Management: The process of identifying, assessing, and mitigating risks to protect investments and achieve optimal risk-return trade-offs.

Portfolio Optimization: The process of constructing an investment portfolio that maximizes returns while minimizing risks based on specific investment objectives and constraints.

Big Data: Extremely large and complex datasets that require advanced tools and techniques to process, analyze, and extract insights.

Blockchain: A decentralized and distributed ledger technology that securely records transactions across multiple computers, ensuring transparency, security, and immutability.

Smart Contracts: Self-executing contracts with the terms and conditions are directly written into code on a blockchain, automating the execution of predefined actions when specific conditions are met.

Tokenization: The process of representing real-world assets, such as stocks or properties, as digital tokens on a blockchain, enabling fractional ownership and increased liquidity.

Algorithmic Bias: Biases that can emerge in AI algorithms due to the quality or bias in training data, leading to discriminatory outcomes or skewed predictions.

Regulatory Compliance: Adherence to laws, regulations, and industry standards to ensure ethical and legal practices in AI investing.

Transparency: The quality of being open, clear, and easily understandable. In AI investing, transparency refers to providing clear explanations of how AI models make decisions or predictions.

Alternative Data: Non-traditional data sources, such as satellite imagery, social media feeds, or credit card transactions, provide unique insights for investment analysis.

Robo Advisors: Online platforms that use AI algorithms to provide automated investment advice and portfolio management services.

High-Frequency Trading: A strategy that uses powerful computers and algorithms to execute a large number of trades in milliseconds, taking advantage of small price discrepancies.

Sentiment Analysis: The process of analyzing and determining the sentiment or emotional tone of text data, such as news articles or social media posts, to gauge market sentiment.

www.ingramcontent.com/pod-product-compliance
Lightning Source LLC
LaVergne TN
LVHW092031060326
832903LV00058B/510